JY   '13

Drawing Fun Fashions

Girly Girl Style

FUN FASHIONS YOU CAN SKETCH

By **Mari Bolte**   illustrated by **Brooke Hagel**

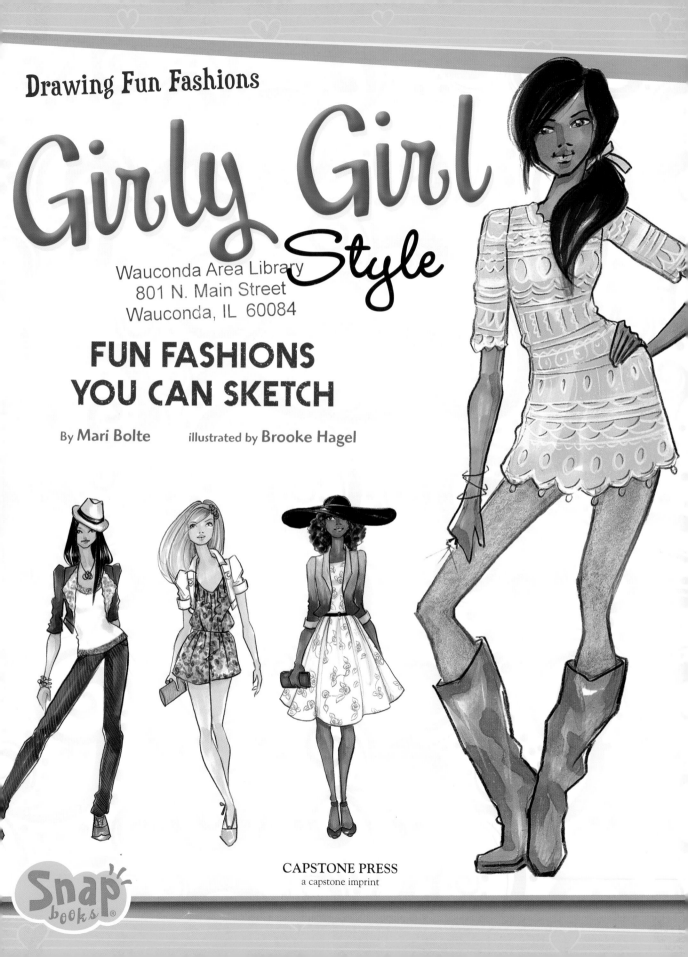

CAPSTONE PRESS
a capstone imprint

Snap books®

Table of Contents

Getting Started

Soft, sweet, and smart are words that describe the typical girly girl—and her wardrobe! The chic and comfortable girl-next-door style is never out of fashion.

Each outfit shows step-by-step instructions on how to draw your very own fashion model. Build upon simple shapes, and use erasable guidelines to create a human shape.

TIP: Blend colored pencils with a Q-tip or blending pencil for softer lines. Try experimenting with watercolor or pastel pencils too.

STEP 1: Start with a simple line drawing. Pick your favorite pose, and use light guidelines to build your model.

STEP 2: Darken the outlines, and start adding in details like hemlines and hand placements.

STEP 3: Erase guidelines, and draw in things such as fabric prints, hair, facial features, and accessories.

STEP 4: Finish any final details and then add in color, textures, and shading to bring your model to life.

TIP: Stick to outlining the models in pencil. Pen or marker outlines will be too bold for this sweet, girly style.

3

Embroidered Edges

A simple tiered dress is accented with a splash of color and some oversized accessories. Color is minimized, keeping the focus on the dress.

TIP: Use a toothpick or the end of a paintbrush to make the dots on the dress.

Radiant Romper

Dresses are great, but sometimes a girly girl needs more freedom. Simple shoes and a sporty jacket dress up this radiant romper.

TIP: Use marker over a dry watercolor base to copy the romper's floral pattern.

BEACH BOUTIQUE

Take your wardrobe on vacation by turning it tropical. An off-the-shoulder peasant shirt and belted denim shorts are the perfect pair for poolside lounging.

TIP: Lace, ruffles, embroidery, beading, or even sequins will make an even more girly impact.

Pretty Prints

Get noticed with bright prints, colorful bangles, and watermelon-colored wedges. Set the outfit off with a mix of accessories ranging from simple to simply stunning.

TIP: Go beyond geometry by trying out other shapes. Fish, flowers, birds, and fruit are other fun fabric choices.

11

Lacy Layers

Girly girls know how to use texture to make their style pop. Lace, embroidery, and faux fur create a rugged yet feminine look. A fedora and oxfords dress up this easy outfit.

TIP: **Use white and light blue colored pencils over dark blue watercolors or markers. Bold strokes will give the jeans a bright sheen. Short, lighter strokes will make the jeans look more worn.**

Crocheted Cutie

Crochet is a timeless fashion choice for the girly girl. Tights and slouchy gray boots complete a look that's totally casual chic.

TIP: Draw the crochet pattern with white crayon. The crayon wax protects the white paper underneath. Even after being painted over with watercolors, the design stays white. This technique is called resist painting.

TIMELESS TREND

Step back to the past with a retro party dress. Add a modern twist with a silky clutch and some sassy sunglasses. Pearls and bows are timeless additions in any decade.

TIP: Choose vintage colors for this dress. If you don't like mustard, try powder blue, mint green, canary yellow, or ballet pink.

Relaxed Romantic

Even the girliest girl needs time to relax and get comfy. An oversized tee, trendy turban, and standout leggings attract attention even at rest.

TIP: Try markers or colored pencils over dry watercolors for added detail.

FLOWERS
Are A Girl's Best Friend

Give the girl-next-door image a makeover. A flirty skirt and updated denim add urban appeal. Keep the look sweet with floral and ribbon details.

TIP: Use a hair dryer to warm the tips of the colored pencils. This will make it easier to blend the layers of the dress.

Style at Sea

Don't get swept out to sea looking like a shipwreck. Sweep through first class like you're the captain of fashion.

TIP: A white charcoal pencil will add detail to the hat brim.

Cold Weather Cool

The only thing warmer than a girly girl's personality is her cool weather gear. Bundle up, but look good doing it! Add plush pieces to create an outfit that's softer than a snowfall.

TIP: Soft core colored pencils will give the jeans a natural, washed look.

A Vintage Affair

Runways around the world have fallen for the Roaring Twenties. Get familiar with the glitz and glamour of the time period. Then add your own modern girly twist.

TIP: Eyeshadow is a neat tool to use for anything puffy or furry. Use a regular foam applicator and cheap eyeshadow to create the soft lines of the purse.

ON THE RUNWAY

TIP: Regular household products make great blending tools. Try:
- nail polish remover
- rubbing alcohol
- baby oil
- cotton makeup pads
- cotton swabs
- soft fabric or leather

A flouncy white dress is ready for the runway on its own. Get more attention with an over-the-top hat and a blended jacket. Fashion week never looked this good.

Extra Accessories

Use your creativity to create original accessories for each outfit. Each piece will reflect your personal style and taste! Take your time and figure out what works for you. Don't forget that accessories complete the outfit.

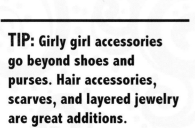

TIP: Girly girl accessories go beyond shoes and purses. Hair accessories, scarves, and layered jewelry are great additions.

TIP: Sketching accessories allows you to make any major changes before adding color.

Read More

Claybourne, Anna. *Accessories for All*. Be Creative. Mankato, Minn.: Smart Apple Media, 2013.

Miles, Liz. *Clothes: From Fur to Fair Trade*. Timeline History. Chicago: Heineman Library, 2011.

Niven, Felicia Lowenstein. *Fabulous Fashions of the 1950s*. Fabulous Fashions of the Decades. Berkeley Heights, N.J.: Enslow Publishers, Inc., 2012.

Internet Sites

FactHound offers a safe, fun way to find Internet sites related to this book. All of the sites on FactHound have been researched by our staff.

Here's all you do:

Visit *www.facthound.com*

Type in this code: 9781620650356

Super-cool stuff! Check out projects, games and lots more at **www.capstonekids.com**

Snap Books are published by Capstone Press,
1710 Roe Crest Drive, North Mankato, Minnesota 56003
www.capstonepub.com

Library of Congress Cataloging-in-Publication Data
Bolte, Mari.
  Girly girl style : fun fashions you can sketch / by Mari Bolte.
    pages cm — (Snap. drawing fun fashions)
  Summary: "Lively text and fun illustrations describe how to draw cool fashions"—Provided by publisher.
  ISBN 978-1-62065-035-6 (library binding)
  ISBN 978-1-4765-1774-2 (ebook PDF)
1. Fashion drawing—Juvenile literature. 2. Girls' clothing—Juvenile literature. I. Title.
  TT509.B6525 2013
  746.9'2083—dc23   2012028365

Editorial Credits
Lori Bye, designer; Nathan Gassman, art director; Marcie Spence, media researcher;
    Laura Manthe, production specialist

The illustrations in this book were created with marker and pencil.

Design elements by Shutterstock.

Printed in the United States of America in North Mankato, Minnesota.
092012   006933CGS13